i

c

o

p

e

CCM Design & Cover by *Michael J Seidlinger*
ISBN - 978-1-937865-43-6

For more information, find CCM at:

http://copingmechanisms.net

SEAN H

THIS MUST BE THE PLACE

DOYLE

For T, and KA

Every atom, every molecule, every group of atoms and molecules, however simple or complex, however large or small, tells the story of itself, its pattern, its purpose, through the vibrations which emanate from it...Thus at any time, in any world, a soul will give off through vibrations the story of itself and the condition in which it now exists.

—Edgar Cayce

These are my memories of the ghosts of myself. Be they real or not, they have made me, put me here, kept me alive and continue to do so.

12 Elliot Drive, Hicksville, New York, June 1st, 1976 —

I am in the car with my mother and little sister when a tornado cuts across our block and throws our car into a neighbor's yard. My little sister is thrown from the back seat into the back of my head and then into the dashboard. My mother hits her head on the steering wheel. I am fine, not a scratch. When the tornado picks us up everything goes still and quiet, even though the car — a huge Plymouth Fury III — is spun and then hurled as if made out of papier-mâché. My mother becomes afraid to drive in the rain.

The Willow House, 3rd Ave and McDowell Road, Phoenix, June, 1994—

I come here after my shift at the record store and sit around at picnic tables outside, scribbling into notebooks while drinking shitty coffee and waiting for my girlfriend, Velvet, to get off work so we can go get high. The crowd here is varied: AA people alongside art people and punks alongside dirty Deadheads and downtown casualties. There are many open mic poetry events, usually outdoors at dusk. One night I decide to read. I go to the mic and drop weapons. I go to the mic and read about Kuwait City and southern Iraq. I go to the mic and read about prostitutes and hashish and drinking homemade wine made out of grape juice in the middle of the Indian Ocean. I go to the mic and curse over and over again. Nobody claps. Nobody moves. I am not asked to read again.

2035 E Turney, Phoenix, December 31ˢᵗ, 1999 —

The turn of the millennium and I am with my father, his wife, and her eldest son. I have swallowed five valium and have been drinking straight whiskey while we all watch Dick Clark on the television. For weeks, the world has been anticipating some kind of Y2K madness to occur. As soon as the clock strikes midnight I go outside into the street and light a joint and start to yell "WHERE IS YOUR JESUS NOW? WHERE IS THE END OF THE WORLD? WHERE ARE YOUR DAUGHTERS TO TAKE ME TO HEAVEN?" and people start yelling back at me as I pull on the joint and my father's wife's eldest son comes outside and just stares at me. I extend my hand and offer the joint— which is dusted, as always—and he just shakes his head and goes back inside.

West Valley Camelback Hospital, Glendale, AZ, Fall 1988—

During the intake, the nurse starts asking me about drugs and lists them off one by one as I nod my head or say "yes" or "no" when appropriate. My mother is crying. I am being admitted to this place because I asked for help because I felt as though I was about to harm myself, begged my mother to get me in because I was sure I was going to kill myself. My mother's tears hurt me and the nurse can see all of this happening and she puts her hand on my mother's shoulder and asks her if she is okay.
"Would you be okay if your kid begged you for help and then you find all of this out about him?"

Jack in the Box drive-thru, Flagstaff, January 9th, 1994—

Shawn and I are very high and sitting in his truck in the drive-thru and he keeps on freaking out and saying things really quietly that do not make sense to me at all. The girl working the drive-thru has made a mistake and forgot his milkshake and he is angry and he is high and he is berating her now—words loosing from his maw in rapid succession with escalating violence and intent to injure—and she closes the window to go fix her mistake and the snow is falling faster and thicker. Shawn reaches between his seat and the gear shift and pulls a huge handgun out and looks me dead in the face and says "fuck this bitch, I am going to shoot this fucking bitch in the face and we are going to drive away" and I immediately feel terrified and elated at the same time. The girl working the drive-thru window sees the gun but opens the window anyway and then throws the milkshake in Shawn's face and it explodes all over him and all over the handgun and all over me and Shawn screeches the tires to pull away and he loses control of the truck and we end up sideways in a snowstorm, laughing like rabid dogs.

Home, 14418 N 52nd Street, Scottsdale, All through the '80s —

My sister and I became latchkey kids as soon as we moved to Arizona. We'd walk each other to and from school, which was just down the block. As we grew older and apart, I would get home from school before her — if I even went at all — and I would get high and then start calling both of my parents at work as Carlos. Carlos was a character I created who spoke like a stoned *cholo*. For some reason, my parents never spoke out loud about Carlos.

Jones Beach, Long Island, New York, August, 1977 —

My mother took me and my sister to the beach with a friend of hers, a woman she used to work with. The woman is very kind to us and looks out for us and lets us play with her dog. When we finally go out into the water we're both bitten over and over again by giant horse-flies, every time they land they pinch and snap and my sister starts to cry and my skin starts to get red and splotchy. We go back to the towels and chairs where our mother and her friend are and they are talking quietly and my mother puts calamine lotion on both me and my sister, but then we all start getting dive-bombed by the horseflies and we go back to my mother's friend's house for lunch. While there, I hear on the radio the reports about The .44 Caliber Killer and how he is terrorizing all of New York City and how he is targeting and killing young couples and I get scared and ask my mother if she is scared and she says "I'm not scared, Seany."

David Berkowitz is arrested two days later for being The .44 Caliber Killer.

Warren 24th Apartments, 3024 N 24th Street, Phoenix, AZ Summer, 2002 —

Living in this rent-by-the-week SRO is a nightmare but it beats sleeping in parks. Maggie contacted my grandmother and told her I had been on the streets for a long time and the two of them devised a plan to get a roof over my head. I am so fucked up from protecting myself and trying to feed myself that I end up with pneumonia. My friend Chris comes over to make sure I am eating and drinking enough water and he brings me an old TV and an old Playstation and a small sack of weed to try and bring my spirits up. We sit around smoking and playing NASCAR games and I start to feel more and more like a human being again. The other residents of the apartments are all destitute and shady, even more than I have become. They talk shit to me in the laundry room and when I am walking to my apartment and one of them flashes a gun at me one night and tells me he is going to kill my cracker ass.

One night a very drunk man smells weed coming from my apartment and tries to claw his way in through the window and when he pulls the screen off and finally has his arm inside of my room I stomp on his arm until I hear it break. He starts screaming and then the police and paramedics come and when they ask me why I stomped on his arm I tell them that he had been threatening me and had tried to break into my place twice before, which wasn't true, but felt true and felt safe. I do not feel bad about this lie.

SEAN H. DOYLE

Blitz 777, Scottsdale Road and Thomas Road, Scottsdale, May, 1988—

When there are no punk rock shows, we all go to Blitz. Blitz is an all-ages teen dance club. We can smoke inside and kids from all over the valley come to be with other kids with the same sensibilities and terrible fashion sense and the burning need to be seen by members of the sexual orientations they so desire. We watch girls and boys in too much white make-up and black velvet capes twirl one another around the dance floor while an unseen DJ spins "Bela Lugosi's Dead" into "Fashion." We smoke cloves and sneak pulls from bottles of gin or chug bottles of cough syrup and we try to hook up and we snort amphetamines in the bathroom and we get handjobs in old VWs in the parking lot from girls and boys who live across town and aren't involved in our core group of morons.

I wasn't there the night the skinheads came. I wasn't there when they hid under parked cars and attacked people with bats and flashed knives and hit girls and boys and it turned into a riot in the middle of the street.

For years and years, I lied and said I had been. But I wasn't.

20

Deep in the desert off of I-10 and Miller Rd, West Phoenix, AZ, Summer, 2000—

We—Isa, Jesse, Caitlin, and myself—are out here because we are boiling the skin off of some ostrich legs so that Jesse can learn about their innermost workings because he is trying to build some mechanical legs, wearable replacements for disabled people. Real future now shit. Jesse is a genius. Probably one of the few I will ever know. I drove out here with a 55 gallon drum strapped into the back of my truck and now we've built a fire and put the drum in it with the legs and lots of bleach. Jesse brought the guns with him—a .45, the AK-47, a pump shotgun—and I am pretending like this isn't triggering anything inside of me. I take the AK and destroy so many things, raking bullets everywhere as the casings fly free and hot and bounce off my arms. Caitlin crouches down like a baby kangaroo and fires the AK and it knocks her down. The smell of the deteriorating ostrich legs is overwhelming. I can still smell it years later, any time I smell remnants of something having been bleached.

Lindbergh Field, San Diego, May 12th, 1996—

I can see my sister and her friend Alison headed toward me as I step off the plane and I can see that my sister is destroyed and it confirms what I felt during my descent into San Diego— my mother has died. My mother has died on Mother's Day. My mother has died and I wasn't there, I was in Phoenix, at my shitty job. My sister grabs me and sobs into my shoulder, "I'm so sorry, mommy is gone," over and over again into my shirt, her tears burning my skin. I hold her and look at Alison because I cannot look anywhere else. My hands are shaking and my heart is a mess and then I go numb. My mother has died.

Somewhere on the streets of Hong Kong, July, 1991—

A bunch of us went to go see *Terminator 2: Judgment Day* while on liberty in Hong Kong. We have been floating around for months now, all of us going a little more insane with each passing day. The movie theater is unlike movie theaters in the states—you can smoke in the theater and waitresses come around selling beer and snacks—and we are all enjoying ourselves. The movie is a nice distraction. We all get hammered. Huddy and I are the worst of us, neither of us capable of walking without stumbling and neither of us caring at all. We are trying to find a strip club but none of us can really figure out what part of the city we are in, so Border asks a local kid on a scooter and the kid gets irate. Suddenly a whole gang of local kids on scooters are surrounding us. I pull out my dick and piss in a trash can while quoting dipshit lines from the movie and staring at the scooter gang. They disperse and we go on our way. I step into the street without looking and feel someone grab my arm and yank me back toward the sidewalk as a double decker bus goes flying by. Huddy.

Racquetball Courts, Horizon High School, Scotts-dale AZ, July 1987 —

I have been high before but I have never been this kind of high where my eyes will not stay open or focused and where my legs feel like jellyfish and my limbs feel like they are being held down by some unseen force. I am with Tara, a girl I used to make out with behind the synagogue at Temple Chai, and we have been sitting in the sun in the concrete cave of the racquetball courts, smoking pot out of a tiny waterpipe/bong thing and everything is light or lack of light or random light flickering and her voice and her hands slapping my face and her screams punching my ears. Tara helps me to my feet but I stumble and take us both right on down to the concrete again. The sun is setting but the only way I know it is because my skin feels cooler in the air than it did before we started getting high and making out like dumb kids. Tara finally helps me to a stairwell—the very same stairwell me and some of my asshole friends put another kid's Volkswagen in out of spite—and we start to climb up, to try and filch some of the air conditioning from the doors to the school. Instead, I fall. I fall and bounce my head on every concrete step. I try to rise. I hear footsteps and mumbles. I lose time.

12 Elliott Drive, Hicksville, June 24th, 1977—

It is my sister's birthday and everyone is in the backyard and my father is grilling hot dogs and hamburgers and my sister is happy and the whole family is with us and then the bees happen. My sister steps into a hole in the ground in the yard and the bees swarm out and start to sting and attack her and she is shrieking and my mother runs over to grab her and everyone else scatters but I stand and stare at the welts forming where she has been stung and then my father pushes me out of the way and pours a can of gasoline into the hole and calmly drops a lit cigarette into the hole. I watch as bees fly up and out of the hole in flames while my sister screams and my mother screams and my father nods his head at me and says quietly, only to me, "burn anything that ever hurts you."

Souper Salad Restaurant, 2045 E. Camelback, Phoenix, 1999—

Cindy is an older woman I hired to wait tables in the evenings. She has another job—she is a press operator, which endeared her to me when I saw her application—and she is a responsible adult. It only figures that Cindy be the one to lead me to the cult. It takes her a while to step into the breach and bring it up to me, but for months she asked the right questions and witnessed the right things from me. Cindy asks me so casually, referring to it as a "religious studies group," and telling me I can "come and go as I please." Of course I go. Why wouldn't I go?

Albuquerque International Sunport, November 25th, 2005 —

When I land in Albuquerque there is nobody to greet me. I go out to the curbside pick-up area and still nobody. I call my stepbrother's cell but there is no answer. I wait, figuring he might be a little late. I smoke and pace. I try to call again, still no answer. I finally, after doing my best not to, call my father's wife. She answers immediately and tells me her son is not coming to get me and how dare I expect him to drive he cannot see at night and how I should just take the shuttle to Santa Fe. I tell her there are no more shuttles for the night and then the phone goes dead. I go inside and rent a car and call my stepbrother again. This time he picks up and gives me directions to his house. I am exhausted but I drive through the cold desert night. I get pulled over entering Santa Fe. I am still a little drunk from my flight and definitely chalked-out on the Xanax, but I explain to the cop why I am in town and he practically leads me to my stepbrother's house.

Western Dental, 1820 N. 75ᵗʰ Ave, Phoenix, 2002 —

I lied to the oral surgeon and told him I was allergic to morphine because I didn't want to get the urge to hunt it out after, so he ended up crushing and breaking and extracting my broken wisdom teeth without any pain medication. I told him the truth when I told him that lidocaine has no effect on me after years and years of abusing cocaine, so I felt almost everything he did to me. I felt like I deserved it all, like every shooting pain was something I had earned, like every bolt of lightning from my brain was a punishment due for past misdeeds. When he was finished I felt as if none of it was real and the endorphins surging through my body misled me into thinking I could ride the bus all the way home without incident. My mouth was bleeding so much that I had to keep spitting blood into an empty soda bottle and someone on the bus saw me and started freaking out and I had to explain to the driver what had happened and by the time I made it all the way home all I could do was smoke bowl after bowl of pot until I passed out.

Grand Street MTA Station, Chinatown, NYC, July 2005—

I had just piled a bunch of my grieving friends into cabs to get them to their hotels scattered across NYC after we'd spent the evening drowning ourselves in liquor after our friend Keith's wake. Everyone was shitfaced—my friend Allen even pulled a knife on the cabbie after I pushed him into the front seat with him, to show the cabbie he was from Texas—and I was no exception. I stumbled away from Motor City and made my way—somehow—to the subway station to catch the D back to Bensonhurst. I was so drunk I could not feel my teeth. I stood on the platform and started to sweat the liquor out of myself. I picked up a paper on the bench and it was all in Chinese and I got mad and then I started to take off my shoes. A woman was standing fifteen feet away, watching me, clucking her tongue. I took off my shirt, yelling about handjobs and death and how members of my family had just robbed me of half a million dollars. I took off my pants right as the train pulled in, waving them around so my wallet and money went flying everywhere. I tried to bend down and pick up my things as the doors to the train slid open and the rush of cool air engulfed me. I draped my pants over my shoulder and put my shoes on my hands and when I tried to grab my shirt I saw the woman who had been clucking her tongue had it in her hand and she and a man from inside of the train helped me get on.

I woke up on the platform at Coney Island.

I still could not feel my teeth.

Aboard USS Nimitz CVN-68, South China Sea, [CLASSIFIED]—

We are in the middle of a typhoon with forty-four foot swells which are tossing this massive ship around like a toy in a bathtub. I have been watching shipmates stumble through passageways with trash bags in hand, puking into them and losing balance everywhere. All aircraft have been brought into the hangar bay and secured and the ship's company has been directed to stay inside of the ship until we are out of the storm. I slowly make my way to an observation deck on the island and go outside, lashing my wrist to a railing with my belt. I watch the sea roil and foam. I close my eyes and feel the power of the sea and I think about how small I am, how small I will always be, how if I somehow go overboard it will take days to be found or even be noticed to be gone.

West Valley Camelback Hospital, Glendale, AZ, Fall, 1988—

Every time I open my mouth, Raymond calls me a faggot. Raymond is my roommate. Raymond has a lion's mane of hair and hand-poked tattoos on his hands. Raymond is fifteen years old. He is here for reasons he refuses to discuss and he is probably the most hyperactive and volatile person I have ever met. The windows in our room are safety windows and they are thick. Raymond likes to crouch down by the door like an Olympic sprinter and then explode, running full speed headfirst into the plate glass window. Raymond also likes to walk up and down the halls with his dick hanging out of his fly. Nobody says anything to the staff because they all think Raymond is crazy—hilarious, considering we're all in here for being crazy—and they are afraid of his temper. After thirty days, when I am being discharged and released into the wild, Raymond finally speaks to me without malice.

"I've been here a year. You're the best roommate I ever had. Don't fuck up out there, faggot."

Some steakhouse joint in Santa Fe, New Mexico, December 2005—

I am sitting at the bar of a restaurant my stepbrother's partner manages and I have just told the bartender to try and make sure there is liquor in my glass at all times. I am here helping my father die. I am here helping my father die while trying to help everyone around him accept his death. I have a belly full of Xanax and I am guzzling whiskey and I want—no, need—someone, anyone, to touch me. All I am burning for on the inside is kindness and flesh. I keep trying to get the bartender's attention. She knows my father is dying. She is being kind. I keep trying to talk to her. I ask her if she wants to go outside and smoke a joint. She does.

My disconnection from my body is terrible and it hurts so I ask her, politely, if she has a man. She says no and smiles at me, but I know that it is a pity smile, a smile reserved for the deranged or the dying. We are passing the joint back and forth and I can taste the difference between my whiskey-soaked saliva and hers, brimming with softness and beauty.

Back inside, I start flirting with her again. My stepbrother is sitting next to me, drowning his own feelings. He knows everyone in Santa Fe, so a parade of people come up to give their early condolences and he introduces them to me and they give their early condolences to me as well and I thank them. I watch as the bartender watches me. I take two crisp hundred dollar bills and cup them in my palm. She walks over.

"If I give you money—this money—will you take me into the walk-in cooler or your car or anywhere but here and let me make out with you, let me maybe put your nipples in my mouth for a few minutes? I just—I need so badly to feel alive and to feel another human being's skin right now."

My stepbrother's partner took me outside and hugged me, telling me never to do such a thing again. When we went back to the place the next night, the bartender was gone. Four days later, so was my father.

Fisherman's Wharf, San Francisco, January, 1993—

On liberty from the Nimitz, an old hippie tries to sell me and Curley hits of acid. Curley has been drinking from a bottle of Rumple Minz and tells the man to give the acid to the sea lions and leave us alone. I have been drinking whiskey. I copped a joint off of a young dude with dreads. Curley gets pissed off and calls me a stoner and then wanders off to go yell at the sea lions. I make my way over to him and can see the signs already—Curley is going to be sick—and prepare myself. Curley wobbles and tries to climb over the barrier to go be with the sea lions, so I grab him by the waist and pull him back down to the deck.

"Doyle, man? I think I'm gonna be fuckin' sick."

Curley stands up and runs into a t-shirt shop on the boardwalk and I try to keep up with him. He isn't even in the door all the way when he shouts that he needs a bathroom. The elderly Asian man tells him to get out and then it happens. Curley erupts all over racks of t-shirts, his vomit filling the air with heat and stink. The elderly Asian man runs over and starts hitting Curley while pushing him toward the door. Curley pukes on him, too. I am high and

SEAN H. DOYLE

buzzed and laughing. This scene has happened in many different places, always with the same result—I end up having to carry Curley back to the boat.

Dad's Apartment, Santa Fe, December, 2005 —

Trust me when I tell you that there is nothing more brutal in this world than trying to hold up your father while he shits into a portable toilet attached to a walker and he is basically shitting into a plastic grocery bag.

The Holy Oratory, Undisclosed Location, Phoenix, 2000—

Dr. Bruce has left me a detailed message about picking up Heather before class. He has been trying to push us together for a while, having me give her rides home and telling her she can call me when she has questions about what we are studying. Heather is really great, but always so meek/cautious and I feel like she is coming to Dr. Bruce to find answers, whereas I am coming to confirm answers. Dr. Bruce told me in confidence that Heather's beau, who has been in prison for over a year for multiple DUI arrests, is not only a smart person, but a terrible person for Heather. I can do simple math.

Monte Vista Lounge, 100 N. San Francisco Street, Flagstaff, AZ, January 8th, 1994—

There is a very angry and strange man at the bar who keeps muttering to himself about my friends. He makes some comment about a "white Bob Marley," in reference to my friend Brian who has awful dreads but is the nicest guy in the world. The man knows that I hear him. I am drinking straight whiskey and I make a point of raising my glass in his direction and making a show of dragging my index finger across my throat. He sidles up next to me and grabs hold of my sideburn and says "Happy Elvis' birthday, motherfucker" as he pulls on it. I reach beneath his arm and push two rigid fingers under his ribs and into his meat, and then I grab the ribs and pull toward myself, hard. The man lets go of my face and tries to recoil but I have him and pull him even closer. I lick the side of his face and say "maybe you should buy me and my friends a round, cowboy?" and let go of him. He apologizes and buys a round and then quickly leaves the bar.

Later that night I fall asleep crying in the dark on the floor of the basement because I wanted the man to have a knife or a gun and for him to kill me.

Ham's Restaurant 3302 N. 24ᵗʰ Street, Phoenix, Summer, 1998—

My father is choking on a sandwich. Everyone around us isn't paying attention but I am sitting across from him and I see his face turning and his eyes watering. He glances up at me and looks panicked but I act as though there is nothing wrong and sip my Jack and Coke. He kicks me under the table and I finally act as though I see what is happening to him. I push his plate and glass away from him to the floor and it raises the room to a different state of awareness. I push him back flat against the wall behind him and punch him in the chest, hard. His eyes pop and whatever was stuck in his throat flies free and hits the table with a wet thud. Everyone else at the table—his wife, some other folks who are ghosts now—suddenly show concern for how hard I hit him, as opposed to recognizing that I probably saved his life. I get up from the table and go to the bathroom and dig my house key into a packet of cocaine and snort two ridiculous lumps of it into my face and go back to the table.

Home, 14418 N. 52^(nd) Street, Scottsdale, 1986 —

This dude I work with told me and my bud-
dy Dave he could get white crosses for super
cheap so we told him we'd sell them for him at
our school. He gave each of us big baggies of
them, hundreds of caffeinated amphetamines
and dust in the bags, me with visions of extra
cash and people coming to me for a quick high.
Dave paid the guy but I didn't have any cash so
he fronted me the pills and I was supposed to
pay him back. It was no more than forty bucks,
really. Weeks go by and I have hardly sold any
and I have been crushing them and snorting
them with this girl I am seeing and then one
afternoon the guy shows up at my house all
angry, yelling at me for his money. I tell him I
don't have any money and go get him the rest
of the pills and he suddenly has a bat in his
hand and is threatening me and I start to laugh
and ask him if beating me up over forty bucks
is a good idea and then he just leaves. I was
fucking terrified.

4434 N 22nd Street, Apartment 4A, Phoenix, Late May, 1996—

My mother has been dead for less than two weeks. I cannot sleep so I listen to Art Bell's Coast to Coast AM all night while chain-smoking and crying and masturbating. Art Bell keeps on talking about things like remote viewing and shadow people and I am a mess so I start to let my mind unravel. I am late on my rent. I am about to lose my job. I have been sporadically fucking a coworker at my directory assistance call center job. I have also been sporadically fucking a friend's wife. I try to call Art Bell's show but my phone is disconnected. I go out onto my patio and sit there and watch the sun rise, putting out cigarettes on my thighs. I pray for death to come soon.

Kitsap Mall, Silverdale, Washington, September, 1990—

I am in a shitty chain bookstore trying to buy books for my first time at sea. They have nothing that interests me—no Henry Rollins, no copies of Maximum Rock and Roll, no fLiPsIdE, no Ginsberg—so I ask the girl behind the counter if there is an underground type store around where I can find the things I am actually looking for. She smiles and says she will be right back and I wait. She comes from the back room with her backpack and hands me a small book. Steven Jesse Bernstein. The small book is called Personal Effects. She tells me it will blow my mind and destroy me. She asks me if I am in the Navy. I tell her that I am and then she invites me to come back in an hour when she is done with work and we can talk. I should have gone back.

Eddie's Grill, 4747 N. 7th Street, Phoenix, Spring 1997—

I am out of cocaine. My coworker Johnny has cocaine and says he will give me some after work before everyone goes to the drag show. I go to Johnny's apartment after work to share his cocaine. Johnny takes a shower. I find a compact disc jewel case on the coffee table covered in powder. The lighting is bad. I cut myself two huge Sean-sized lines. I snort them. It is immediately apparent that it is not cocaine. I feel sick and woozy. I feel lightheaded. I panic and crawl into a closet, pulling jackets and blankets down on top of me while crying. Johnny finds me underneath his clothing, weeping. Johnny calls me a greedy idiot and tells me I have just snorted enough ketamine to kill men larger than I am. I panic some more and beg Johnny to help me. He gives me two valium and draws me an ice cold bath, adding ice from his freezer. Everyone else shows up in drag. One of the servers, Ward, looks like exactly like *Mrs. Doubtfire*. Ward gets in my face in the tub—where I am naked and crying and everyone is gawking and laughing at me—and calls me a greedy junkie piggy.

175 Bay 41ˢᵗ Street, Bensonhurst, Brooklyn, 1975—

I was very little and it was raining and I had just been woken up by my parents to be shuffled into the car to go home. I was on my father's shoulders with a Spider-Man comic in my hand. My grandmother kissed me goodbye. My vision was full of the steps—concrete and wet and cold—as I went flying toward them. I had waved the comic in front of my father's eyes as he missed a step and down we went. I heard my name being screamed and felt the impact of my skull on the concrete and then everything went fuzzy and warm. I woke up the next day surrounded by melted ice packs and a stuffed Spider-Man. My mother blamed my father, saying he was drunk.

Homeside Acres Apartments, Central Phoenix, Summer of 2001 —

My stepbrothers and I decide enough is enough and we band together in an intervention for my father and their mother. We all come together and meet with an addiction counselor, ambushing the two of them. I cry, begging my father to please not die on me, sharing with him how empty I feel from my mother's death in '96, how his accelerated drinking is a slow and legal suicide. His wife calls me a hypocrite and a coward, mentioning my own drug use and cocaine overdose from '98. My stepbrothers talk about how important my father is to them and I feel guilty because their mother is not important to me. My stepbrothers are being good men and I am being a selfish boy. My father and their mother enter into separate rehabilitation facilities—hers, because she is insured, is nice and modern—across town from one another and—his, because he is uninsured is a run-down ramshackle place full of men on parole and men with missing limbs—they are both terrified to be apart.

I argue and bicker constantly with one of my stepbrothers after the other goes back to New Mexico. While my father and his wife are in the drying-out clinic, I develop a strange and awkward sexual relationship in the laundry room one night with another tenant at the apartment complex. Her husband turns out to be a notorious local serial killer and gets caught later on, after I've left the desert and gone back to Brooklyn.

McDonald's, Paradise Valley Mall, Phoenix AZ, Fall of 1988—

I am sitting at a table with Todd and Dave and we are all trying to eat our Big Macs but we all have numb throats from the cocaine we just snorted in Todd's Suzuki Samurai while he drove like an idiot trying to flip it over. The news had just reported a recall on the vehicles because they were not stable and had a tendency to tip over when taking turns faster than 25 miles per hour. Todd took turns in the parking lot at speeds far exceeding the warning the news people wanted the world to heed. I like Todd but I have never trusted Dave because Dave hangs out with people who are total dickheads and has a habit of being kind of a bully to people even though he appears to be permanently stoned. Todd is quiet and funny and even when he tries to hide his heart is shows through whatever black shirt he is wearing that day. Later on when we are back in class after our break is over, I cannot feel my tongue and Dave turns around at his desk and hands me the vial of cocaine and tells me to go to the bathroom and do some more if I want. I thought it was Todd's cocaine, so I handed it back to Dave and just sat there, letting my numb tongue rattle around and explore in my numb mouth.

Aboard USS Nimitz CVN-68, [CLASSIFIED]—

When people have beef with one another, we seal the hatches on our living quarters and break out the boxing gloves. All of the tables and chairs get cleared from the lounge area and everyone gathers around and watches the fights. There are rules: two minutes to a fight, two men to a fight, no hitting below the belt or behind the head, a fighter can quit by raising both arms above his head and the other fighter must respect that, a knockout is a knockout is a knockout, both fighters must drop whatever brought them to this place as soon as their fight is over, no bragging, no post-fight bullying, all fighters must hug it out upon completion of the fight.

21 Elliot Drive, Hicksville, Long Island, New York, 1976—

In the basement, I am caught playing doctor with the twins by their father. He sees me on the floor with his naked twin daughters, sees my hands, sees their faces. He rushes me and I am little and stupid but I know that if he catches me it will be worse than my own father catching me because he is yelling words I do not understand and the girls are terrified. He lunges for me and misses and I run as fast as I can to the stairs. He throws a barstool and it explodes behind me on the stairs and I race up and into the storm door, crashing through it and running as hard as I can for my own house, less than half a block away. The garage door is open and my father is in there working on his '73 Firebird—the one that will eventually end up "stolen"—and I run by him into the house. I hear yelling and more yelling and my heart is fast and I am scared and then I hear something crash and then I do not hear any more yelling. I never go back toward the twins' house ever again while we live on that block, and my father never says anything to me about it until years later, when he is dying.

Scripps Memorial Hospital, 9888 Genesee Ave, La Jolla, CA, April, 1996 —

My mother is in a coma because the radiation treatment weakened her colon so much that a portion of it burst and went septic. The doctors found some strange bacteria in her body and because of this anyone who goes into the room to be with her has to scrub up and wear medical scrubs. I have just returned from my mother's dentist after getting a broken tooth pulled and my mouth is full of bloodied gauze and I do not say anything to my mother's nurse about it because I am not going to let some bacteria get in the way of me spending time with my mother while machines are breathing for her and she is dreaming of another life. I pull out the bloodied gauze and put it into a trashcan next to the bed and sit down and hold my mother's hand and tell her about my life, about how at night I go to the strip club near the Sports Arena because none of the women there will ask me how I feel or what I feel or anything of the sort and I can be alone there at a table in a darkened corner and the music is loud and the cokes are ice cold and I can disappear.

The Holy Oratory, Undisclosed Location, Phoenix, 2000—

For months I have been bathing in so much information flying around like loosed electrons. I have been learning about The Brotherhood of Light, studying the Egyptian mystery schools, getting a crash course in aspects of Zoroastrianism and Gnosticism, reinforcing my understanding of Kabbalah, and have been soaking every part of my mind in Hermetic astrology. Dr. Bruce has done my natal chart and passed it to everyone in the group. They all know me in ways I have yet to master, and this bothers me, feels like my interactions are tainted. In study, Dr. Bruce begins to defer to me when it comes to anything close to Judaism. Cindy has begun to resent bringing me to the group, as Dr. Bruce likes to immediately jump on her when she speaks or has a question. The tension during mass is thicker than the incense. Dr. Bruce can feel that I am about to leave for good. This is when he begins to push me, to leave messages on my machine, to send emails full of long and confusing essays about the future and my role in it.

Brian's father's house, West Phoenix, Summer, 1989—

I am hiding out at Brian's father's house because I got into it really badly with my mother. Brian's father is a nice enough man. Brian is my best---and probably at this point, only---friend. Brian is a diabetic. Brian's father is a diabetic. Brian's father has a "cleaning lady" who comes by one afternoon when I am hiding out in Brian's room, stoned, listening to music. The "cleaning lady" is actually an escort who pretends to clean the kitchen while topless. I watch the whole thing through a crack in Brian's bedroom door. Brian's father has a very small erection and she keeps on waggling the feather duster on it and he makes a cooing sound like a ticklish baby. She sucks him off and he has a very loud orgasm less than three minutes later. Brian's father hands her an envelope and she leaves. I never tell Brian what I saw.

Outside the Marriott Hotel, Dubai, United Arab Emirates, July 1992—

We—three of my shipmates and myself—are in a taxi trying to convince the driver to take us to a house of ill repute. The taxi driver says he knows of no such things in his city and we—three of my shipmates and myself—get all manner of belligerent. People are yelling. The taxi driver is laughing at us. Killer—one of my more intoxicated shipmates, a stocky little murderer from Detroit with birth control glasses and a voice like Luther Vandross—is in the back seat, singing loudly about how he is going to puke. I am sitting next to the taxi driver in the front seat and I watch him remove a wad of what appears to be hash from a pouch and pop it into his mouth. I pull out a can of long-cut Skoal and offer it to him. He opens the can and sniffs it, puts it into his tunic, and hands me the rest of his pouch of hash.

"I'mma puke, y'all. Motherfuckers, I said I am going to fuckin' puke up in this goddamn cab in this goddamn pussy-less country!" Killer yells, his head in his hands. We—two of my shipmates and myself—roar at him, chanting for him to puke. The taxi driver says that if Killer pukes in his car, he will leave us by the side of the road. We are nowhere near where the ship is, in fact, we are suddenly in a part of Dubai that looks much like the bombed out warzone we have all come from. Killer pukes. Killer pukes and it flies from his gaping mouth into the back of the taxi driver's turban, splashing over the seats and all into my lap. The taxi driver yanks the emergency break and immediately starts yelling for us to get out of his car. The taxi driver opens his door, and then I do it, I turn in my seat and kick him, full force in the ass away from the car, all while sliding over and slamming the door and taking off with his taxi. We left it at The Marriott. I tossed the keys to a Commander in uniform and told him to get the fucker washed because there was puke all up in it.

Dad's Apartment, Santa Fe, December, 2005 —

The stillness and silence of snowfall is my best friend right now. I go out onto the back patio of the apartment to smoke and I keep the curtains open and I watch my father as his body drowns and I can hear the oxygen tank even out here with the snow falling on my head and I smoke and I look at the moon.

I want to switch places with him.

Aboard USS Nimitz CVN-68, [CLASSIFIED]—

We're at General Quarters for a drill and I am running to my station on the flight deck when I see a bunch of people standing around white as sheets and then I notice all of the blood and there is a body sticking out of a hydraulic weapons elevator shaft with no head and the floor and the sailors are covered in blood.

SEAN H. DOYLE

*7-Eleven, Scottsdale Road and Shea Avenue, Scotts-
dale, AZ, May 1989—*

A bunch of us are in two different vehicles,
coming back from seeing the movie Heavy
Metal. Five of the eight of us are on LSD. We
pull into the 7-Eleven to get sodas and bullshit
and smokes. I am sitting in the passenger seat
of the station wagon, with my friend Brian, his
girlfriend Tara, and my friend Nicole, who is
driving. The others pile out of my other friend
Jon's Suburban. Immediately there is shouting.
Three very large dudes come walking up on
them, one of them shoving my friend Scott into
the hood of the Suburban. The three large dudes
are yelling about something being thrown and
hitting their car. My friend Josh says something
back to them and then everything happens in
a blur of limbs and screaming. One of the big
dudes picks up my friend Jon and slams him
into the pavement, headfirst. One of the other
dudes takes a swing at Josh and then they try
to grab my other friend Rick but the big dudes
look over and see the rest of us in the other car
and take off. Brian and I try to get out of the car
but the doors are locked. We finally get out and
I run into the 7-Eleven and jump the counter
and grab the guy running the place and tell him
to call an ambulance, because Jon is twitching

58

on the pavement. The ambulance comes and so do Jon's parents. I called them, too. His father, angrily, says to me as Jon is being put into the back of the ambulance, "Where the fuck were you, tough guy?" I don't say anything.

I was the one who locked the doors.

Church of Body Modification, West Phoenix, Summer 2001—

Willow and I both have two hooks in our backs attached to ropes and quick-links which are attached to the bumper of a fifteen-thousand pound armored truck and we are leaning forward and sweating and laughing and trying to get the thing to move. We rock back and forth in unison—tension in the rope right to snapping and then releasing and moving forward—and the truck begins to move a little bit. At first it feels like it has moved no more than an inch but then we start to churn our legs and everything is moving, the sky, the sounds of everyone cheering and screaming, the truck, hot and thick blood in our bodies. As we begin to run and really move, the truck gets heavier and we can people yelling at us to keep going from up behind us. People had climbed onto the roof of the truck, wanting to feel our energy and participate. We pull the truck over a speed bump and gain momentum and have it moving at a pretty quick pace when we see the end of the lot approaching. We smile at one another and stop, embracing one another with our sweat and our power.

Ocean Beach, San Diego, April, 1996 —

I am sitting in the sand at 2AM and trying to get higher than I already am. The waves are lulling and calming. There is some kind of party happening in the backyard of some bungalow-looking apartments behind me. I can hear laughter and women and men and cheering and more laughter. This weed is not enough for me, I've reached that stage where smoking any more of it is wasteful, so I shove the bowl into my pocket and put myself belly-first onto the sand, which is cool and damp. I turn my face to the side and leave it in the sand and cry. I know what's coming and I know the coma my mother is in will last longer than anyone thinks. I know that being in the room with her is like talking to a ghost, but she is my ghost and she made me, carried me, and I have to be in that room with her. I am willing to burn everything I've ever built for her to live.

*14418 N 52nd Street, Scottsdale, AZ, Christmas,
1988 —*

We woke as a family to a phone call from my
uncle saying that my grandfather had died
during the night. My grandmother had died
from her cancer around Halloween and Christmas was always the most important holiday
for them and my grandfather died of a broken
heart in his sleep. As soon as my father and
mother started talking about my father flying
back to New York that day, I spoke up and said
I wanted to go with him. I felt for my father-
-losing his parents in such rapid succession-
-and wanted to try and be there for him. It
was agreed that I would go with him and my
mother asked me and begged me not to let my
father do anything stupid or hurt anyone with
his anger, especially me.

My father and I sat in the very back of the air-
plane, chain-smoking and not speaking to one
another. My father kept drinking scotch after
scotch and when he fell asleep I took what was
left and drank it myself. When we landed in
New York City we were both exhausted and
drunk and reeking of smoke.

With the Blood and Steel People, Phoenix, 2001 —

Everyone around here carries guns. There are guns in every vehicle, guns on desks, guns in closets, guns in plastic bags inside toilet tanks, guns in purses, guns in the storage room, guns, guns, guns. When people come to my apartment to hang out the first thing they do is remove their gun and set it on the table in front of my couch, where I end up staring at the gun out of habit almost nonstop. None of them really know my history with guns, why they make me sweat, why they make me want to go for a long walk. They always offer to bring me along when they go out to the desert to shoot things and act like Rambo, but I always decline. Nobody needs to see me with a gun. Ever.

*Lipsticks Topless Club, Heroica Nogales, Sonora,
Mexico, August 1996 —*

I am, as Lou Reed put it, "waiting for the man."
The place is dark and damp and there are strobe
lights on a slow cycle which make it seems like
I am in and out of consciousness. The girls
look like wolves. Their handlers look like rats.
The man I am waiting for is a man who is supposed to sell me five pounds of Mexican brick
weed. I was connected to this man by a former
coworker. The man is an hour late and I am
getting nervous because I think the wolves and
the rats know who I am and why I am there. I
palm a valium copped from a street pharmacy
into my mouth and swallow it dry. The music
in Lipsticks shifts from narco-corridos to Stone
Temple Pilots. I can taste the chalky and alka-
line from the valium and I can see a fat man
working his way slowly toward where I am
sitting. The fat man stops and nods at me and
then quickly points his chin toward a half-open
door to signal me to meet him there.

Inside of the room are four other fat men. All
of them acknowledge me but say nothing. The
original fat man claps me on the shoulder and
says "where is your car, carnal?" I tell him it is
on the US side, parked in the lot near the Mc-

Donalds. The original fat man nods at the others and they all look at me as they leave. "They will meet you there in one hour. Don't fuck this up, okay?"

Nimitz Grinder, United States Navy Recruit Training Center, San Diego, 1990—

EW1 Stockdale is screaming at me. I am pumping my legs up and down within a small portion of the grinder—a giant blacktop that reflects all manner of heat and light and sky and sweats pain—while everyone else goes to chow. I am being reprimanded for falling asleep in a class on fire safety. This reprimand is called a Marching Party, or as EW1 Stockdale likes to refer to it—as MASH—making a sailor hurt. EW1 Stockdale is my Company Commander and he has hated me from the moment I stepped off the plane in San Diego, with my long hair and earring and pack of smokes and me walking up to him—the only man in a Navy uniform I can spot—and asking him, "Hey chief, you know where I'm supposed to go wait for the bus to boot camp to pick me up?" EW1 Stockdale is screaming at me about that very moment, telling me he should have sent me back on the next plane so he could shame my family for giving me life, telling me that the rest of my fellow recruits are planning a blanket party for me, telling me that he would love to fuck my mother in front of me, telling me that I am a waste of my father's jizz, all while I pump my legs and refuse to look into his eyes.

"You're the worst kind of sailor, Doyle. You're the kind of sailor who'd fuck his shipmate without even giving him a reach-around."

I keep pumping my legs.

Dad's Apartment, Santa Fe, December, 2005—

My sister and her husband have come from San Diego. They will not be here long, and I feel awful and terrible for my sister. She does not know these people, does not know my father's wife or her sons, does not know this tension, this anticipatory ache in the room. My father's eldest brother is still here and he does his best—as I do—to buffer this tension. My father asks my sister's husband to come closer to him and he does. My father—barely able to keep his eyes open, barely able to breathe, barely able to speak—mumbles quietly for him to get even closer. He does. My father speaks.

"Do you see this monster? He is my son."

"Yes. Sean."

"I'm dying. If you ever hurt my daughter, he will find you and break your legs. He will break every bone in your body. Because he is my son. Do you understand?"

"Yes."

My uncle laughs. I laugh. My sister's husband laughs.

Ayako, Biltmore Fashion Square, Phoenix, 2001—

We're sitting in a very nice sushi restaurant in Central Phoenix—we being myself, a lizard, a cat, a puzzle, a leopard lady, an evil genius, a psy-borg, and others I am unable to explain— and everyone in the place is acting as if we are all normal, as if nobody sitting at the large table in the middle of the room has altered themselves beyond recognition. Sake is flowing and food is being consumed and a man I met for the first time earlier that day is telling us about the time he had someone perform a surgery to extend the opening to his urethra and they accidentally got silver nitrate in his urethra and he passed out from the pain.

I have no idea how I got here or why.

Phoenix Art Museum, 2002 —

On the days and hours the Phoenix Art Museum was open for free admission, I would get there and spend as much time inside as I could. Air conditioning and silence. I would wander around and act as if I knew what I was looking at, knew what I was there for. I was delirious most of the time. Starving. Usually in the midst of some awful nicotine withdrawal.

One day I found a stairwell that was unlocked and went inside of it and climbed up to find the door at the top locked. When I went back down the door I had come through was also locked. I realized this would be a problem later, but the stairwell was cool and dark, so I used my satchel as a pillow and went to sleep under the stairs. I opened my eyes at one point and saw darkness outside the window and knew I was locked inside the museum — the stairwell — for the night. I slept and slept.

When they found me in the morning I told them I had been locked in the stairwell all day and night and had been knocking to be let out. They believed me and apologized.

Aboard USS Nimitz CVN-68, [CLASSIFIED]—

I would love to tell you about the time the boot camp pilot crashed his F-18 Hornet into the ass-end of the flight deck in the middle of the Persian Gulf during sorties and what happened after that, but that shit is classified. I should not be writing anything about the military. You should not be reading it.

BS West, Central Phoenix, 1997 —

I am sitting in a stranger's car in the parking lot of a bar jerking off while he watches me because he has better cocaine than I do and he promised to give it to me if he could watch me jerk off but I am so flat-lined without any coke in my blood and my cock is raw and half-limp and he keeps on mumbling sweet nothings with a hum that feels evil and like a constrictor of sorts and I cannot get off and he keeps on licking his lips and touching my arm and trying to inch his hand down to touch me and I keep stopping and telling him not to touch me—that wasn't the deal we made—and finally he starts to yell at me and I put myself back into my pants and all he does is give me two little bumps but those two little bumps explode inside of my head and I feel free and I know I can erase what just happened with the right amount of whiskey.

Dad's Apartment, Santa Fe, December, 2005 —

I've been pulling the night shift. I stay up most of the night in the glow of a silenced television and listen to my father breathing with the hiss of his oxygen tank and the gurgling in his chest. His wife has been mostly sleeping through the night, which is a welcome relief. It is very hard for me to pay attention to my father's needs and balance that with my own emotions, let alone anyone else's. I have been reading Murakami's *Norwegian Wood* with one of those little clip-on lights. The book is destroying me, all of the emotion of the story sometimes helping me to somehow escape the roiling seas inside of my heart, the sadness, the commotion. When the sun rises and my father's wife starts to stir, I make a pot of coffee. There is a trick to making coffee when doing hospice work, and it involves crushing up two to five Ativan and adding it to the grounds. It helps me ease into sleep, and it helps my father's wife stay mostly stable while the sun is up.

The Holy Oratory, Undisclosed Location, Phoenix, Easter, 2000—

There are new faces in the room. Some people have come from as far away as Iceland and Germany for Easter, to have mass with us and to break bread and speak. Dr. Bruce is in his liturgical robes and his face glows and his hands are red from making meat pies and beets. As usual, I am wearing all black, a black long-sleeved dress shirt over black undershirt and black jeans and black boots. Dr. Bruce introduces me to the new faces and they act as though they know me and Cindy explains to me in confidence that Dr. Bruce has been talking about me to all of his other students, about me being a natural at understanding charts and philosophies and how someday I might be his teacher. I go into the bathroom and swallow two muscle relaxers. I go into the Oratory where the smoke is burning and the air is still and the room is cramped and everyone is in that state—the beginning of a Latin mass is so still and perfect and you can always feel the vibration building from the toes and through the head—that informs me that today will be different. I close my eyes and feel Dr. Bruce's voice. I rise. We all rise. We all fall down.

The Howlitt's house, 1739 E. Butte Drive, Phoenix, Summer, 1985—

I am supposed to be hanging out and acting like a big brother to Eddie, who is three years younger than me and a pain in my ass. Our families are close because my sister is a member of his mother's baton twirling troupe. They are all up north, at camp. Eddie and I spend most of the day out front trying to skate. He is better than me and I resent it. I go into the house to get some water and find myself in his sister Andie's room. Andie is a senior. I go through her drawers and check out all of her panties. I put two of the sexier pair into my pockets. I go back out and skate with Eddie some more and then we get into a fight and I bloody his nose. Later that night, I jerk off into a pair of Andie's panties. I am not even attracted to her.

Scripps Memorial Hospital, 9888 Genesee Ave, La Jolla, CA, April, 1996—

There is another family in the ICU who has someone they love also in a coma. I have been watching them. We have unspoken moments between us, knowing looks and eye movements meant to convey empathy and understanding. When they fall asleep in the waiting room I cover them with blankets. I never sleep. When I go outside to smoke one of them always follows, but smokes further away. Rituals occur when death is hovering, rituals and understandings and unspoken truths.

The day they lose their matriarch everything finally hits me full force in the chest. All of this is real. All of this sitting around and waiting is something inevitable, a death to come, a death to release the ill and to free the waiting from the waiting. I watch them all as they cry and hold one another and watch as they thank the doctors and nurses and all I can think inside of myself is that I know I will never be that graceful or grateful.

I will always burn.

Eddies' Grill, 4747 N. 7ᵗʰ Ave, Phoenix, 1997 —

You never realize cocaine has taken over your life until you start doing really stupid shit. I am doing stupid shit. I am starting to sneak around and do stupid shit like leave the apartment at three in the morning to go meet up with one of the dishwashers who works at the restaurant to buy a sixty piece and sneaking back into bed without a sound and then rising before work and shoving fingerfuls of powder into my nose in the shower and then putting two or three lumps of the stuff into my espresso before my shift starts and then going down to the wine cellar and snorting lines off of my hand and sharing it with a waitress and we laugh and laugh and everyone knows what we're doing and it's all such stupid shit.

Aboard USS Nimitz CVN-68, [CLASSIFIED]—

The Count was from Philly. He let everyone know this whenever he was upset about something—"I'm from Philly!" flying loose from his maw in his nasal tone. We called him The Count, lovingly, because he looked just like The Count from Sesame Street. He wore his nickname with the same pride he spoke of his hometown. Whenever we were in port somewhere, you were guaranteed to see The Count holding court in some awful dive bar with no less than two local prostitutes at his side. The Count was a baller, a king.

The Count was pissed at me for stealing his fuckbooks [what we called porn] and taping photos from them all over his rack and locker. He decided he wanted to call me out and fight me. Everyone started placing bets and everyone started to go crazy. I didn't want to fight The Count. I liked him and didn't want to hurt him. They sealed the berthing space and moved all the furniture and gave us each our gloves and everyone went dead quiet. A guy named Patterson broke the silence—"Where you from, Count? Show Doyle where you from, son!"—and the space filled with testosterone and whoops and hollers. The Count slapped his gloves together and came at me. He was tiny and quick and that little fucker kept getting up into my ribs and body with his quick little hands and all I could do was hit him on the top of his head and then he caught me with an uppercut and I went to sleep.

Stepbrother's House, Santa Fe, Late November, 2005 —

I am sitting at a desk in a room covered from wall to ceiling in Star Trek memorabilia, all of it still in original packaging, and I am using a computer with enough spyware and adware on it to make it crawl to load a simple banner image. Every thirty seconds or so another image of gay porn pops up — men engaging in acts and acts engaging in men and all of them beautiful all of them fit and delicious and seemingly free from emotional torment — and I close them as quickly as the browser will allow. I am cruising Craigslist for someone to touch, someone who will touch me. Santa Fe is a wasteland, full of hippies and astrologers and rolfers, hardly any mention of anyone looking for a casual night fumbling around in the dark with a broken man who is taking care of his dying father.

Church of Body Modification, West Phoenix, Summer 2001—

The Blood and Steel People are trying to start a church. They want it to be a place that can defend those who chose to modify their bodies against discrimination. I keep on telling them that calling it a church isn't going to be a good idea. I keep on telling them that unless there is counseling available for people considering having heavier work done on themselves, some kind of guidance and some kind of talk about spiritual or transcendence, calling it a church is a misnomer and a lie. Endless debates and meetings and then a charter is written. They start to ask for donations from the vast community online of body modification people. Money comes in, support. Then someone gets arrested for a procedure. Then everyone panics. Then it becomes a scandal. I had already dipped out by then, but I could've told you what was going to happen.

AZP Skatepark, Flagstaff, AZ, December 1995—

Grass has come up to Flagstaff to play a show with Julia—an incredible screamo band from San Diego—and Primitive Tribes—a local Flagstaff band made up of peace punks and crusties. The show is inside of a skate park and the skate park has no heat and it is thirteen degrees. As always, our second guitar player, Reid, couldn't make the show. This has happened three or four times now. I am very close to quitting the band, but I love playing with Brian and Anthony, so I put up with Shawn's weird mope shit and persevere, for the rock action. A band of hessians show up at the skate park and beg to get put on the bill. They're on tour from the Midwest and just want to play a show. They're called Ritual Device and seem like nice enough dudes. We let them go on before us. They destroy everything and everyone in the place with a solid and guttural Jesus Lizard-like sludge and stomp. I wish I was in that band and on that tour. We play our set and every animal comes out of my body and there is steam rising from my hands on the fretboard and I run halfway up the halfpipe and slide down on my knees while playing and Shawn is mewling and Brian is thumping and Anthony is pounding and I leave my body with the animals and never notice the blood from my frozen fingers until after, when I can feel every sting.

Greenwood Cemetery, 4300 Imperial Ave, San Diego, May, 1996 —

They say a parent should never have to bury their child. My grandmother — the epitome of class and dignity my entire life — is now burying her daughter, my mother. She already buried her husband not long after I was born and stayed a widow. I am angry because we were all told to keep my mother's illness from her, to keep her unaware at my mother's insistence. Now here we all sit, in the office of a funeral home director and my grandmother is holding her chin up behind dark Jackie O shades and baubles on her wrists. My sister is silent and zoned out. My aunt and uncle keep speaking for everyone until I tell them, again, that I had a conversation with my mother years earlier about death, and about how she didn't want to be buried, she wanted to be cremated. Everyone starts to bicker until my grandmother speaks up for me, reminds everyone that I am my mother's firstborn, that if anyone would know her wishes, it would be me. My sister nods. My aunt and uncle start to speak again and my grandmother shuts them down with a look.

Dad's Apartment, Santa Fe, December, 2005 —

A woman comes to the apartment to say good-bye to my father. She is apparently someone he sold a car at his job, but his wife is acting as though this woman is someone more important, someone she does not want in her home. I hang back and watch from the kitchen as the woman leans into my father in his death chair and speaks to him. My father's wife hovers around with a vibration and glow that is transparent to me. The woman acts unaffected and says her goodbyes and then leaves. I watch my father's wife pour herself a scotch and feel her as she seethes.

Part of me is not-so-secretly pleased to have witnessed this happening.

Los Olivos Park, 28th Street and Glenrosa Avenue, Phoenix, 2002 —

The tricky part about sleeping in parks is not getting caught by the police and also not being a nuisance to the few people who dare come out into the scorching sun to use the parks. This is why I mostly slept in the parks in neighborhoods where there were minimal children. I slept in parks near nursing homes and retirement communities — both of which are in abundance in Phoenix — and I did my best to be invisible. It is very hard to hide six feet of tattooed male in a park. Oleander bushes worked the best. They shaded me from the sun and they stayed cool at night.

The park I slept in the most was Los Olivos Park. It was mostly unused and the entire border of the park was shaded by olive trees and Oleanders. In the summer it was harder, because of irrigation. The water would fill the park in the night, releasing all sorts of bugs and flooding the bushes. Those were the nights I would sleep anywhere I could find darkness and shelter.

With the Blood and Steel People, Phoenix, 2001 —

Barrett has horns implanted in his forehead
and long, dyed dreads. He is one of the kind-
est people I will ever meet in my life. He and
the rest of the guys working in the machine
shop—Chris, Willow, Eric—are always working, always hustling to make jewelry for bodies
they will never see. Whenever I go out into the
shop I feel better, safer, less worried about being called out for something I didn't know was
on me. Chris and Barrett end up become two of
my closest friends. They help me move after I
lose my apartment after not getting paid for a
month. We hang out together away from work.
We laugh a lot. Sometimes it feels like Steve
and Beki don't want me to be around, don't
want me to be friendly with the other people
under their employ.

Scripps Memorial Hospital, 9888 Genesee Ave, La Jolla, CA, April, 1996—

It continues to feel as though my mother's oncologist is lying to me. Whenever I ask him a question he blanches as if I have stuck him with something sharp between his ribs. The first time we meet he tells me that her colon burst because she was weakened by the cancer and the radiation treatment exploited that weakness. The next day he told me they found some unknown bacteria in her body and in order to see her we would have to scrub in and out and wear protective clothing. I know that she is dying and I know inside of myself that his job cannot be easy, but I cut loose some words upon him that aren't compassion-based and I leave the hospital to go sit outside and cry and smoke. From that point forward, he no longer speaks to me, only to my sister or my mother's sister.

Enlisted Club, Puget Sound Naval Shipyard, Bremerton, 1993 —

Curley and I are drunk and playing pool at the bowling alley and he is yelling at some guy who keeps going over to the jukebox to "play some fucking metal." I keep on laughing because this is what Curley does when he is loaded. He goads people and fucks with people and then acts like a lump of sugar when they confront him. The guy goes back to his stool at the bar and a Garth Brooks song comes on and Curley is livid and starts yelling about being Navajo and how country music is an affront to his people and the guy stares through Curley and spits on the floor. Curley walks over to him and cracks him in the head with his pool cue and the guy falls down and then Curley takes his pool cue and shoves it under the felt on the table, ripping it and yelling, and then he stomps off, leaving me there to deal with it all. For once, he stood up for himself and didn't puke.

The Holy Oratory, Undisclosed Location, Phoenix, 2001 —

This is how I finally get free. We are all in the middle of class and things are getting heated. Heather's boyfriend has been released from prison and he is practically sitting on top of her on the couch and we are all discussing sin and the concepts of sin and the proscriptions of sin through time and space. Heather's boyfriend keeps slamming his fist on the table while smiling whenever Dr. Bruce asks me a question. Each time he does it, everyone tenses up. Cindy is sitting on the floor next to the table and she clenches her face and then stares at the top of the table. The room is thick with smoke and incense and everyone is drinking wine but me and I am laughing inside at the macho display of a man who just got out of prison. That's when it happens, when Dr. Bruce spews the line that ends it all for me, the line that takes everything I learned and sets it to burn in the sky in front of my face. Dr. Bruce starts off talking about family bloodlines being poisoned by the sin of those who came before, talking about how if a man in my family was a rapist, some generations down the line it would balance out by someone in my blood being raped. I laugh but nobody else does.

"Do you know what Down's Syndrome is, Sean?"

"Yes."

"It's what happens to a family who has done something so unconscionable that God decides to smite them with a child who cannot feel anger, who cannot reason with anger, because God is angry."

The switch inside of me flipped and that was it for me. I never went back and stopped returning emails and stopped listening to messages and stopped reading charts and stopped it all.

Stepbrother's House, Santa Fe, Late December 18th, 2005 —

My father has been dead for less than three hours and I am loaded on whiskey and pills and weed and playing pool in my stepbrother's garage and we are all feeling relief even if we are too afraid to say so. My father's wife is sitting on a milk crate and drinking and crying and talking nonsense. I am playing pool against the stepbrother I am trying not to hate and he says something to his mother about a website and donations and I am unsure if I hear him correctly so I ask him to repeat what he just said. Everyone gets quiet. He tells me he set up a "memorial" site for my father where people can make donations for his mother. Inside of myself, I am going insane and I see myself grabbing him by the throat and thrashing him around until he is a ragdoll. Because I am loaded and grieving and feeling trapped, I start to yell at him and I yell that I am going to break his neck. He rolls his eyes at me which makes me even angrier and I start yelling nonsense and my other stepbrother's partner comes over to me and he engulfs me in a hug so big and so warm that I collapse.

Marina Cortez, 1880 Harbor Island Drive, San Diego, May, 1996 —

I do my best to stay straight for the services, which are held at the marina where my mother worked. The Rabbi we found in the Yellow Pages is wonderful and kind and very gregarious. I sit between my father and my sister, holding their hands, feeling the electrical currents inside of them wavering. My mother's boss speaks about her in beautiful in lovely ways. Some of her friends as well do the same. It is my turn to speak, to give my first eulogy. I rise and tell everyone how much my mother meant to me, how her kindness and care was something I learned and hoped to carry with me always. I spoke of her tolerance for my antics as a teen, and how she encouraged me always to be the best person I could be. The Rabbi laughs and refers to me as "Zalmen," which is my Hebrew name, "the good son." I sit back down and my sister squeezes my hand at the same time my father does. I fight the tears. I fight them.

Kelly's Apartment, Central Phoenix, 2002 —

J let me sleep on his couch a few times when this homelessness thing first started. I never asked him outright, he would just tell me to get into his car and we'd go to his place and smoke weed and then he'd go to bed and I would crash. Very rarely did he let me stay there when he was out. He let me use his shower, made sure I ate something.

After a few weeks of uncertainty I was staying in the spare room of the friend of an ex. J came over one night to pick me up and hang out. He arrived with the little sister of my ex, who he was apparently dating. Then he hurt me. He stood in front of me as I sat on the couch, telling me he couldn't believe how helpless I was, how fucked up I was, and how he was sure that it wouldn't be long until I put a gun in my mouth and killed myself. He said all of this to me and I just stared at him and cried. A grown man, crying.

ACKNOWLEDGMENTS

The sitting down and writing the book part is solitary, but that's not all that happens. Birthing takes more than eyes and fingers. Without the following people, this would all still be stuck in between my head and your hands.

Love and respect to Michael J. Seidlinger for believing. You are the last true believer, my brother. Thank you.

Thank you to the towers of song Joe Riippi and D. Foy. You have both done so much for me and I love you. Thank you. Keep rockin' and pushing words.

Thank you to the music made by Michael Gira, BELLS≥, Greg Sage, and Duff Egan. None of this would have happened without hours of losing myself in your notes.

Thank you to my psychic twin and other set of eyes, Wendy C. Ortiz. You bring light and kindness to the world and I can never tell you enough how much I appreciate your presence in my life.

Thank you to Tobias "Paddington" Carroll and Jason Diamond of Volume 1 Brooklyn for believing and being incredible human beings.

Thank you for being my sister and friend, Carrie Pick. Thank you to the O'Shea clan. Thank you to my brother, Jordan Ginsberg. Thank you to my other brother, Steve Shodin. Thank you to Jim Ruland. Thank you to T Kira Madden. Thank you to Penina Roth. Thank you to Leesa Cross-Smith. Thank you to Robb Todd. Thank you to Daniel Long. Thank you to Daisy Genna. Thank you to Daniel Nester. Thank you to Sylvia Jung. Thank you to Teebs. Thank you to Juliet Escoria. Thank you to Cari Luna. Thank you to Ty Hardaway. Thank you to Hannah Miet. Thank you to Leah Umansky. Thank you to Dolan Morgan. Thank you to Natalie Eilbert. Thank you to Joanna C. Valente. Thank you to Dena Rash Guzman. Thank you to Zach Barocas. Thank you to Mishka Shubaly. Thank you to Vicki Nerino. Thank you to Jessica Freeman. Thank you to Upright Coffee in Greenpoint for keeping me fueled and ready for battle.

Thank you to the love of my life, Theresa Adams. Your support and love and kindness helps keep me going and believing. You are the greatest gift. I can only hope to be half the human being you are.

Thank you to The Gracie for being the best dog in the world.

Sean H. Doyle lives in Brooklyn, NY. He works hard every day to be a better person, and is learning how to love himself more. **www.seanhdoyle.com**

This Must Be the Place is his first book.

OFFICIAL
CCM ◖

GET OUT OF JAIL
* VOUCHER *

- -

Tear this out.
Skip that social event.
It's okay.
You don't have to go if you don't want to. Pick up
the book you just bought. Open to the first page.
You'll thank us by the third paragraph.

If friends ask why you were a no-show, show them
this voucher.
You'll be fine.

- -

We're coping.

◖

CPSIA information can be obtained
at www.ICGtesting.com
Printed in the USA
FFOW05n0152040116